A prototype Land-Rover: a version from about 1965 of the lightweight air-portable model that entered service in 1968. In production there were minor changes, including the substitution of a standard wire grille. The weight had been pared down to enable the fully laden vehicle to be carried by a Westland Wessex helicopter.

FOUR-WHEEL DRIVE AND LAND-ROVER

Nick Baldwin

Shire Publications Ltd

CONTENTS

Published in 1997 by Shire Publications Ltd, Cromwell House, Church Street, Princes Risborough, Buckinghamshire HP27 9AA, UK. Copyright © 1988 by Nick Baldwin. First published 1988. Second edition 1997. Shire Album 221. ISBN 0 7478 0342 0.
All rights reserved. No part of this publication may be reproduced or transmitted in any form or by any means, electronic or mechanical, including photocopy, recording, or any information storage and retrieval system, without permission in writing from the publishers.

Printed in Great Britain by CIT Printing Services, Press Buildings, Merlins Bridge, Haverfordwest, Pembrokeshire SA61 1XF.

British Library Cataloguing in Publication Data: Baldwin, Nick. Four-wheel drive and Land-Rover. – 2nd ed. 1. Four-wheel drive cars. I. Title. 629.2'222. ISBN 0 7478 0342 0.

Editorial Consultant: Michael E. Ware, Curator of the National Motor Museum, Beaulieu.

ACKNOWLEDGEMENTS
The pictures are mostly from the author's collection and in many cases originally came from the vehicle manufacturers concerned. The Rover Group deserves special thanks, as does David Shephard, who took the cover photograph and helped in other ways. The excellent library at the National Motor Museum, Beaulieu, provided invaluable assistance in writing the captions.

Cover: *One of the first: a Land-Rover 1948 model owned and restored by Andrew Stevens.*

Below: *Various ways were tried to give 4 x 2 vehicles adequate off-road potential in the early years of the twentieth century. B. J. Diplock studied elephants before making his Pedrail wheel, shown here on a steam traction engine.*

This is said to be a 4 x 4 Spyker of 1904, photographed at Brighton in 1905. It has the typical features of the Dutch car, including the elaborate dust shields under the chassis and the circular radiator and bonnet with louvres. Although the shields and rear competition number make it difficult to see details of the transmission, there is certainly a live axle as opposed to chain drive at the rear.

THE ORIGINS OF FOUR-WHEEL DRIVE

We are all familiar with the transmission arrangements of the average family car. Its engine drives either the front or rear wheels via a differential, which allows one wheel to turn more or fewer revolutions than its mate when cornering. Without the differential each driven wheel would skid to compensate for the different distance that it had to cover on a corner when compared with the wheel attached to the other end of its axle. Whilst the differential is invaluable on hard surfaces, on soft ones it effectively makes a car have only one-wheel drive because all the power tends to go to the wheel that is meeting the least resistance : in other words the wheel that is spinning helplessly.

Four-wheel drive (4 x 4) is a straightforward system of feeding the engine power to both front and rear wheels by revolving shafts. (The original military term '4 x 4' implied four wheels, all four driven, double-tyred wheels counting as one.)

However, as in the case of two-wheel drive (4 x 2) vehicles, it is possible for one wheel to spin on each axle and effectively immobilise the vehicle. To avoid this happening some 4 x 4s have differentials that can be locked to force equal power to all wheels. Many 4 x 4s can be driven on the road as 4 x 2s, which indeed they need to be if there is no differential between the shafts driving the front and rear axles. The explanation for this is that, just as wheels on opposite sides of a car travel different distances, so do the front and rear wheels. Thus, a vehicle in permanent four-wheel drive with no central differential would soon scuff its tyres bald. A third differential might permit all the power to go to the least resistance and make just one wheel spin, so once more a lock is provided. With all the differentials locked solid a 4 x 4 becomes genuinely four-wheel drive and is virtually unstoppable.

One tends to think of four-wheel drive

3

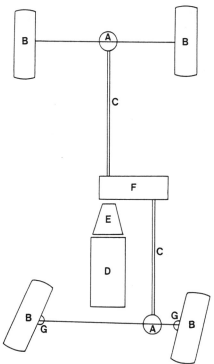

Four-wheel drive. A, Housing for gearing to provide right-angle distribution of power and containing a differential (sometimes lockable). B, Wheels: note that the front ones adopt different angles when steered. C, Propellor shafts. D, Engine. E, Gearbox. F, Transfer box giving option of 4 x 2 or 4 x 4 or else containing a third differential and providing permanent 4 x 4. Usually a second ratio is built into the transfer box to provide crawler gears for slow off-road use. G, Constant velocity joints to allow simultaneous drive and steering.

as stemming from the Second World War. This was when all-wheel drive first came into widespread use but the origins of four-wheel drive date back to the dawn of motoring. Burstall and Hill's steam carriage, built in Leith in 1825, had optional four-wheel drive and the famous French designer Amedée Bollée took up the idea fifty years later. Gandon built a 4 x 4 steam lorry in Paris in 1900 and internal combustion-engined examples achieved fame in 1903 with the remarkable Spyker racing car from Holland.

Until then four-wheel drive had been used simply to increase traction on rough

tracks and fields: after all, very few proper roads existed. Even in 1914 only 3296 miles of North American roads had hard surfaces, compared with over two million without. The Spyker, however, was intended for metalled roads and four-wheel drive was chosen to ensure that the power from its 8.7 litre, six-cylinder engine was put to maximum use when accelerating and cornering.

It was to be fifty years before these matters were to be considered seriously again by designers. In the meantime it was off-road ability or the need to keep vehicles moving in snow and mud that took priority. Most interest was shown in the United States. Battery electric 4 x 4 trucks were available from Couple Gear and Quadray in 1904; these makers soon added petrol-engined generators to increase range. However, it was to the Badger that most early credit goes, despite the fact that the Duplex, in Badger's home state of Wisconsin, may have been a little earlier.

German immigrants William A. Besserdich and Otto Zachow built a steam-driven 4 x 4 car in 1908 and then built a 45 horsepower Continental four-cylinder petrol-engined Badger in 1909. It could carry seven passengers at up to 55 mph (89 km/h) on good surfaces yet crawl through quagmires impossible for all but light horse-drawn vehicles. It had the advantage of four-wheel braking via the transmission at a time when the vast majority of cars had only two-wheel brakes. It also had double reduction axles and a third differential that eliminated wind-up in the transmission between front and rear axles. This differential could be locked if the ground conditions became difficult.

Ten of these cars were built by Badger, which had become the Four Wheel Drive Auto Company. FWD was soon to find true success in the field of trucks, but not before it had sold one of its 1912 cars to Mr Pinkerton of the famous detective agency.

Similar to the FWD forward-control truck, but with the addition of steering on all wheels, was the Rambler (later Jeffery and then Nash) Quad which appeared in Wisconsin in 1913 and by a tenuous route of company changes of ownership was to be an ancestor of the Jeep. Another early American maker was Walter, whose first 4 x 4 appeared in 1911 and whose name still

Petrol-engined Badger cars were built in Clintonville, Wisconsin, United States, from 1909 by the forerunner of the Four Wheel Drive Auto Company. This is the first, still preserved at the firm's museum. It had the nickname of 'The Battleship' because it was nearly unstoppable.

A petrol-electric bus in use in Vienna in 1911. It had Lohner-Porsche electric motors in four wheels, which made it ideal for towing the passenger trailer in icy and snowy conditions. Note the chute for sand to help the solid-tyred rear wheels grip.

Britain was generally slow to adopt four-wheel drive, partly because its railway communications were so good and partly because many roads had hard surfaces. However, the technology existed, as this 20 horsepower Standard, built for the Delhi Durbah of 1913, goes to prove.

exists on snow-ploughs and crash tenders for airfields.

Meanwhile, in Europe Georges Latil of Marseilles had developed in 1898 a driven front axle that was used initially for attachment to existing horse-drawn vehicles. From this it was but a relatively small step to add drive to the rear axle as well. Exactly when this took place is uncertain but 4 x 4 Latils were in widespread use during the First World War. These Latils were shaft-driven but Ferdinand Porsche developed a system in 1898 which employed separate electric motors in each wheel and thus simplified the transmission of power.

Germany and Austria favoured four-wheel drive for military purposes and as early as 1905 Austro-Daimler was offering heavy gun tractors with all-wheel drive. In 1906 German Daimler made shaft-driven 4 x 4 tractors and lorries, in 1907 Mercedes made a large 4 x 4 car for use in Africa and in 1910 Ehrhardt made a 4 x 4 gun carriage. From 1911 Chatillon-Panhard made

gun tractors in France and in Australia the Caldwell Vale Motor and Tractor Construction Company made forty massive 4 x 4 lorries from 1910 to 1912 for the peaceful purpose of opening up the outback.

Equally pacific in intention was the fleet of 4 x 4 cars built by Standard of Coventry for use on a royal visit to the Delhi Durbah in 1913. Based on the 20 horsepower high-ground-clearance Colonial Standard, they looked just like normal touring cars until the drive to the centre of the front axle was noted.

Though the Standards were light enough to use pneumatic tyres, most of the heavier types of 4 x 4 vehicle had iron or solid rubber tyres, which inevitably limited their grip. To overcome this they used strakes or chains when working in soft conditions.

Probably the first heavier 4 x 4 truck to make pneumatic tyres standard, in 1917, was the vehicle that became known as the Oshkosh. It was made by William Besser-

In 1898 Georges Latil developed a self-contained front-wheel drive power pack which was originally coupled to existing vehicles. Soon complete front-wheel drive or four-wheel drive vehicles were built for him by Ets Charles Blum at Levallois and tractors by Ets Tourand. This is a 1913-14 example.

dich after he left FWD in 1913. At that early stage he was beginning to despair that four-wheel drive would ever be commercially viable. The total of six FWD cars and five trucks sold in 1912 had been disheartening, and the total of nineteen trucks in 1913 was little better. A surprise order for fifty trucks for the British Army came too late to influence William Besserdich's move. Subsequent output by FWD in the war years 1914-18 was a remarkable fifteen thousand vehicles.

The Italian Pavesi was developed in the First World War and was subsequently adopted by Fiat. At first it had a two-cylinder engine but it had acquired a four-cylinder unit by the time that this one (shown with snow-plough blade) was built in the mid 1920s. Because it pivoted in the middle in order to steer, the wheels followed each other's tracks and the machine was virtually unstoppable, particularly when strakes were fitted to the rims.

In 1923 French's Motor Engineering Works in London built this Anzani-engineered 4 x 4 with Wrigley gearbox to the design of a Belgian named Hollé. It could steer on all wheels and employed a central transfer box from which four shafts passed direct to bevel gearing in each wheel hub. Little more was heard of the ingenious vehicle until 1926 when Vulcan made a larger Hoverta Vulcan version.

THE FIRST WORLD WAR AND AFTER

During the First World War 4 x 4 vehicles were used extensively for the first time. They were used for carrying supplies and troops and for towing guns in the appalling conditions of mud and destroyed roads. Germany and its allies tended to use four-wheel drive for their largest vehicles, whereas Italy, France and the United States made relatively lightweight and manoeuvrable 4 x 4s. One of the most interesting designs emanated from the Italian Ing Pavesi and consisted of a two-cylinder, short wheelbase machine which steered by pivoting the two halves of its frame in the middle. It was a universal pivot that also allowed the wheels to keep in even contact with the ground, however bumpy. Fiat ultimately took over this design.

French makers like Latil, Renault and Panhard made relatively small numbers of vehicles because of the conflict within their country and Britain concentrated on producing as many conventional 4 x 2 three-tonners as it could. As a result it was left to FWD, and its licensees, as well as the variously named Quads and lesser rivals, to fill the breach. Tens of thousands were delivered, despite early problems when some of the inhabitants of Wisconsin, long a favoured state for German immigrants, did their own bit for the war effort by sabotaging the 4 x 4s being sent to the Allies in Europe.

When the war ended many military vehicles went on to serve civilian functions and for a long time an industry existed in England (FWD at Slough) and France (Labourier) reconditioning 4 x 4 chassis and fitting them with new equipment like

Most requirements for off-road vehicles in the 1920s were met by 6 x 4 designs. Above is a Renault staff car with twin tyres all round for extra flotation on sand. Another way of improving off-road capabilities is shown by the Morris-Commercial (below) converted to half-tracks by Roadless Traction.

Above: *An American FWD of First World War origin shown in service in London in the 1920s. The FWD was an important design which met most needs for off-road civilian vehicles in the 1920s in Europe and America. Note the original wooden wheels: these were gradually replaced by steel types on FWDs in Britain.*

Below: *The first Oshkosh of 1917, made in the town of that name in Wisconsin, USA, is dwarfed by another all-wheel drive Oshkosh, a J series 6 x 6 tractor built for desert use in the 1970s.*

tipper bodies and snow-ploughs (and ultimately building substitutes from new components). The Latil, with four-wheel drive and four-wheel steering, as well as the Pavesi, went on to serve as timber winches and tractors. Most other new types of 4 x 4 vehicle were effectively stifled by the wartime surplus.

Thornycroft, in England, made a few 4 x 4 Hathis in the mid 1920s and Scammell offered all-wheel drive later in the decade, but most emphasis shifted to 6 x 4, a cheaper and simpler way of providing useful off-road capability. For even more difficult conditions half-tracks at the back of cars and lorries were developed by several firms, notably by Roadless Traction in England.

Little attention was paid to light 4 x 4 vehicles, though a most ingenious design from a Belgian named Hollé was built experimentally by French's Motor Engineering Works in London in 1923. It had an Anzani engine and a central transfer box from which four drive shafts radiated direct to each wheel, all of which steered. The idea was taken up in the Holverta Vulcan of 1926 and was later seen in certain Italian 4 x 4s.

Unfortunately there was little commercial demand for 4 x 4 vehicles, which were inevitably relatively costly and complicated. Military demand was minimal and, though undeveloped territories were being opened up overseas, it was to 6 x 4s and half-tracks that most of the work was entrusted. The British Colonial Office had come to an arrangement with 23 countries to share the cost of some off-road trains in 1927. These were hauled by Leyland and AEC 8 x 8 tractors, but few were built, it proving more economic in the longer term to use aircraft or to build proper roads or railways.

Gun tractors and lorries were made by several firms for Germany and its allies in the period leading up to and during the First World War. This is one of Ferdinand Porsche's designs on test in 1914. It could tow a 30.5 cm Mauser and had an 80 bhp engine.

Marmon-Herrington's all-wheel driven vehicles were often Ford-based, as in the case of this personnel carrier made for Persia. The firm was run by Colonel Herrington and the brother of the maker of Marmon luxury cars. By using cheap and freely available components they were able to bring four-wheel drive within reach of many new customers.

THE 1930s AND SECOND WORLD WAR

The 1930s commenced with interest in all-wheel drive at a low ebb. The world economic recession favoured the production of cheap and basic vehicles and this was the era of widespread mass production of standard motor cars. Specialist firms eked out an existence with orders for road-building, snow-ploughing and cable-laying vehicles and cheap, light cross-country vehicles tended to be of the half-track variety typified by the Citroen-Kegresse.

In an effort to provide competitively priced 4 x 4 vehicles in the United States, Colonel Arthur W. Herrington began to convert Fords. His firm, Marmon-Herrington, started with heavier types in 1931, using the former Duesenberg factory for production. The Ford conversions became big business in 1936: by then re-armament in the United States and Europe was causing increased interest in

many types of off-road vehicle. The Latil 4 x 4 had remained in production in France and in Britain the local FWD firm had been acquired by AEC. A direct descendant of the reworked American FWDs would ultimately become one of the most famous vehicles of the Second World War: the AEC Matador.

In Italy Fiat acquired most of its competitors, amongst which was OM, which had itself acquired an outstanding 4 x 4 from Ansaldo in 1932. This was the Autocarro designed by Giulio Cesare Cappa in 1928 and sometimes called the Autocarretta da Montagna. It had a 1.6 litre, two-cylinder, air-cooled engine, independent suspension and four-wheel steering. It was a far cleverer design than that of the famous Jeep, though this received most of the credit for pioneering four-wheel drive in a lightweight form.

Before considering the Jeep it is important to recall that Germany was keenly interested in 4 x 4 cars in the 1930s. Its rearmament was of a rather circumspect nature and, to keep off-road technology high on the agenda without being too overtly military, all manner of cross-country car trials were organised. The fact that the average car club member stood no chance of achieving success unless he had been loaned a special 4 x 4 seemed to have been overlooked by the Allies. In theory the Tempo G1200 was freely available from 1936 and is said to have been sold to some forty countries. Stoewer made a clever 4 x 4 with all-wheel steering and, when this was taken up by the Wehrmacht, BMW and Hanomag helped with its production. Wanderer in the Auto Union group made ingenious six-cylinder 4 x 4 cars from 1933, as did the sister firm of Horch, using eight-cylinder engines.

In the 1930s Mercedes-Benz was one of the most prolific suppliers of both 6 x 4 and 4 x 4 cars, most of the latter having all-wheel steering. Even Japan, which was slow to become a motor manufacturer, built 4 x 4 cars for military purposes. The Mitsubishi PX-33 of 1934 was remarkable in being diesel-powered. Its engine was a six-cylinder 70 bhp unit displacing 4390 cc.

Whilst Marmon-Herrington was stealing the limelight in America, the traditional firms like Walter, Oshkosh and FWD continued to make small numbers of vehicles. As a publicity exercise FWD raced a Miller-engined 4 x 4 car at the Indianapolis 500 between 1932 and 1937. Qualifying speeds of up to 118.4 mph (191 km/h) were recorded but no victories were scored. Even so, it provided a valuable lesson in torque proportioning differentials and constant velocity transmission joints.

The big 4 x 4 event in America at the end of the decade was the emergence of Karl Probst's Bantam. American Austin

Scammell emerged as one of Britain's principal producers of specialist heavy vehicles from the late 1920s. It made several types of 4 x 4 and 6 x 6 vehicles and here one shows off the drive to its front axle and the considerable degree of flexibility allowed by the centrally mounted transverse leaf spring.

13

There was much interest in off-road trials in Germany during the 1930s and most of the country's manufacturers built 4 x 4 cars. Shown here is one from Auto Union (the controlling group for Wanderer, Audi and DKW) being driven by a Nazi Party member (note the swastika armband), aided by a navigator who clung on to straps at the rear to improve traction.

had built the immortal Seven under licence and the US Army had even tested these as scout cars in 1933. The firm had a chequered career, becoming American Bantam in 1936. The Continental-engined 4 x 4 did well in its military trial and 2675 examples were built in 1940-1. Bantam was far too small to make the vast numbers required and mass production of similar vehicles was left to Ford and Willys-Overland. Known as General Purpose vehicles, the initials GP were soon corrupted to Jeep, a familiar character in the Popeye cartoons.

By the end of the war approximately 740,000 Jeeps had been produced. Their mark on motoring history is inestimable because many of these, plus new civilian versions, went on after the war to fill roles that had never before been dreamed of. Their European predecessors and contemporaries were mostly far more complex and therefore more expensive to produce and maintain. As a result they were built in much smaller quantities and had far less impact on the subsequent civilian market.

However, large types of 4 x 4 vehicle produced by General Motors and Ford in Canada and by General Motors' offshoot

Bedford in Britain also had great significance. These were, again, simple no-frills vehicles and hundreds of thousands were ultimately in use, of which no less than 52,245 were the ubiquitous Bedford QL 3 ton model. Bedford had never before made a forward-control vehicle, let alone a 4 x 4, so its achievements were remarkable, even though partly counteracted by the fact that General Motors' Opel factory had been taken over by the German government to make equally potent Opel Blitz lorries.

The Second World War marked a major turning point for 4 x 4. Time and time again all-wheel driven vehicles showed their superiority over conventional machines and henceforth a high proportion of military vehicles would have 4 x 4, 6 x 6 or even 8 x 8. Many of the duties formerly performed by tracked vehicles were now undertaken by wheeled machines. Though in the 1930s most interest had been towards military ends, four-wheel drive had also proved itself to be useful in opening up desert and forest regions in the search for raw materials. This was to be an area of massive expansion in the coming years.

14

Right: *Britain made few small 4 x 4 vehicles before the arrival of the Land-Rover. One exception was the wartime Humber Heavy Utility. This was based on Super Snipe mechanical components where possible and used its 4.08 litre, 85 bhp engine. The gearbox was a two-range four-speed unit and there was independent suspension at the front.*

Left: *The original Jeep was perhaps the most famous light 4 x 4 of all time. Following the successful prototype at American Bantam, versions built by Ford and Willys-Overland were followed by over half a million standardised general purpose vehicles from 1941 to the end of the war. The Jeep had a 2.2 litre four-cylinder petrol engine developing 60 bhp, a three-speed gearbox with high or low range and disengageable drive to the front axle.*

Right: *Nikolas Straussler was a well known designer of off-road vehicles in Europe. He worked for Weiss Manfred in Hungary before bringing some of his prototypes to England, where he acted as consultant to such firms as Garner and Alvis. This is his G1 (Garner) 4 x 4 of the late 1930s with a Ford V8 engine. Similar vehicles were produced in quantity at Morris-Commercial, Guy and Fordson whilst Garner made a small number of heavier 4 x 4 lorries with twin Ford V8s.*

An early compilation shot by the Rover Company showing various Land-Rovers, including the original centre-steered prototype, undergoing tests particularly to show their suitability for agricultural work.

THE UBIQUITOUS LAND-ROVER

Of the dozens of new makes of 4 x 4 that have grown up since the Second World War, the Rover Company's Land-Rover is surely the most widely known and respected. It was, though, by no means revolutionary: as has been described, in the 35 years before the Land-Rover arrived, there had been many designs that were far more sophisticated. However, what the Land-Rover had, and all but the Jeep lacked, was just the right combination of power, off- and on-road performance, ground clearance, strength, weight, carrying capacity, low price and simplicity. Virtually everything that had gone before was too expensive to be of anything but highly specialist use; whilst it may have been superior in some respects it

was ultimately let down by its cost and the difficulty of servicing it or finding spares far from the factory where it was made.

The Land-Rover was deliberately constructed to be worked on by anyone with basic mechanical skills and was initially conceived as an agricultural vehicle that a blacksmith could probably service or mend. Nevertheless, compared with the Jeep, it had, and still has, one feature in particular that places it in a category of its own. That is its aluminium alloy bodywork: this has ensured that examples have survived for forty years, even long after the paint has worn off the metal panels.

The choice of Birmabright alloy (which cost three times as much as steel but was only a third of the weight) seems obvious

16

A view of the Rover works at Solihull in the mid 1950s, showing the moving assembly lines full of left-hand drive vehicles for export. Note the oil cooler in front of the radiator on the vehicle in the middle foreground. These were fitted to vehicles used to power stationary equipment, such as fire pumps.

A very early example of a long-wheelbase Series I Land-Rover with capstan winch amongst the pygmies of the Ituri Forest in the Congo in 1955. The explorers are Hal and Helena Weaver. Land-Rovers soon became standard equipment for such journeys and John Baldwin, the publicity manager at Rover (and father of the author) had a collection of several dozen books describing epic journeys they had achieved.

The original centre-steered Land-Rover prototype running an elevator from its rear power take-off. This was largely a Jeep with its engine and gearbox replaced by Rover units.

in retrospect but at the time it was a decision forced on Rover by its inadequate steel allocation. In material-starved post-war Britain, where earning foreign currency was of paramount importance, motor firms were allocated steel in proportion to their previous export achievements. Rover had typically catered for the British middle classes and had sold few cars abroad. Therefore it needed to use something other than steel if it was to increase output.

The managing director at Rover since 1933, and the firm's undoubted saviour,

A view under a very early Land-Rover showing the offset differentials and a separate power take-off shaft running a belt pulley.

Sir Winston Churchill was one of many notable owners of Land-Rovers. When one was demonstrated to him at Chartwell in 1954 he insisted that the driver take it into a swamp to see what happened when it got stuck. The answer was that smartly dressed Rover directors and staff had to push it out and were showered with muddy water from the spinning wheels!

was Spencer B. Wilks, who had previously run Hillman. His brother Maurice was in charge of engineering from 1931 to 1957. Rover purchased two war-surplus Jeeps and Maurice Wilks was much impressed by their abilities, though as an engineer he was confident that they could be improved upon.

His original prototype was a mixture of Jeep and Rover parts and had a central

A long-wheelbase Series I being used for an unusual purpose, even by Land-Rover standards. It is fitted with a device for hitting golf balls to test their resilience and equality.

19

Before factory-built forward-control models became available Carmichael built some to its own design to accommodate its fire-fighting bodywork and equipment. The basis is a long-wheelbase Series II Land-Rover.

One of Rover's own prototypes for a forward-control 2 ton capacity military model is shown here. Various engines were tried, including the 3 litre straight six from the P5 car.

The British Royal Family have long been users of Land-Rovers. This one, built specially for ceremonial occasions, allowed the Queen to stand or sit in the rear. It was photographed before a royal occasion at Edinburgh in 1960.

For even greater cross-country ability, particularly on deeply rutted forest tracks, Roadless Traction modified this long-wheelbase Land-Rover in 1959 to take 10 x 28 tyres. It had hub-reduction axles which reduced its top speed to 30 mph (48 km/h).

21

A 1972 long-wheelbase Series III with hard top at work with the North Eastern Electricity Board in the sort of conditions in which Land-Rovers excel. The newly situated lights (in the wings instead of the grille) were a construction and use requirement. Note the front-mounted winch.

steering position, as befitted an agricultural vehicle. However, subsequent pre-production vehicles had the steering wheel moved to the side, but differed from later Land-Rovers in having a galvanised chassis and a free wheel. This latter feature overcame the transmission wind-up that inevitably occurred if front and rear wheels covered different distances (such as when turning corners) on hard surfaces. A few of the earlier vehicles had disengageable front drive and, after a couple of years, the free wheel was discontinued on the grounds that it added expense and complexity. As with the Jeep, there was a high and low range for the gearbox, though in this case four basic forward gears, giving eight forward and two reverse. The Land-Rover had an immensely strong steel chassis, designed by Olaf Poppe, that used box sections.

The Land-Rover was favourably received at the Amsterdam Show early in April 1948 and in 1949-50 eight thousand were built, over two thousand more than the number of Rover cars in the same period. Half a million were sold by April 1966, a million by June 1976 and by 1988 the total was about 1½ million, with approximately 70 per cent going for export (to more than 175 different countries over the years).

Despite its outwardly similar appearance over more than forty years of production, the Land-Rover changed substantially over this period. The Series I used the Rover 60 1600 cc engine, increased to 2 litres in late 1951. From 1955 a longer-wheelbase version was added and the original short model grew from an 80 inch (2.04 metre) to an 86 inch (2.21 metre) wheelbase in 1954 and then to 88 inches (2.24 metres). This length was standardised for the more rounded-looking and wider-track Series II of 1958, then the long Land-Rover grew from 107 to 109 inches (2.71 to 2.76 metres). A 2 litre Rover diesel had been offered since 1957 and this continued in the Series II in instances when the new 2.25 litre petrol unit was not specified. For the Series IIA the diesel was of the same dimensions as the petrol engine and there were also a forward-control 1½ ton version, heavy-duty normal-control types and all sorts of custom-converted Land-Rovers. In addition there were factory-built station wagons and specialist military types, including a V8-

engined forward-control model from 1975 and a simplified air-portable utility vehicle in service from 1968.

The Series III of 1972 onwards had various new comforts, in addition to an all-synchromesh gearbox, and could have six cylinder and then V8 petrol engines as well as the usual four-cylinder options.

One of the Land-Rover's strengths (as well as a weakness) was its extremely rugged semi-elliptic suspension. This was retained on the grounds that, if a driver was being badly shaken on a rough track, he was likely to slow down before he could damage the vehicle. The success of the Range-Rover had shown that a more sophisticated suspension, though still with beam axles to maintain ground clearance, could answer most of the criticisms, yet still impart great strength. This coil spring set up with double-acting dampers was incorporated in the One Ten model of 1983 and the Ninety introduced in the following year.

The Land-Rover had been produced under licence or by Rover affiliates in many parts of the world. One of the earliest versions was by former luxury car-maker Minerva in Belgium in the early 1950s, followed by Tempo in Germany. In Spain, Metallurgica Santa Ana has made Land-Rover Santana 4 x 4s since 1959, including some models not offered by the original Solihull factory. Santana also makes 4 x 4s of other origins, as befits a firm that in the 1980s became part-owned by Suzuki.

In 1970 the Range-Rover was a brave step away from the basic simplicity of the Land-Rover. Its permanent four-wheel drive required a centre differential to overcome wind-up and its height-adjustable rear suspension, long wheel travel and powerful V8 engine soon established it as a superb on – and off – road performer. It soon achieved cult status with demand vastly outstripping supply.

In 1967 the Rover Company was acquired by the expanding Leyland empire and Land-Rover production reached a record 58,000 in 1975. After that there were many world-wide problems which saw the traditional Third World markets unable to afford the typical 83 per cent of Solihull's output. Indeed in 1992 only 11 per cent went to the Third World, but meanwhile the developed countries' leisure market had expanded dramatically, partly owing to the new Discovery. Whilst this was being developed Land-Rover found itself the jewel in the crown of the potential break-up of the Leyland Group. In 1986, when a turbo diesel became available, JCB, Lonhro, Aveling-Barford, Schroder Ventures and GMC all made tentative approaches, but to keep the volume car

The Discovery in V8i three-door form and as the five-door model introduced early in 1991. The latter in this instance has a 2.5 turbo diesel engine.

23

Left: *At the end of 1990 two hundred examples of an ultra-luxurious 3.9 litre Range-Rover were called the CSK in honour of Charles Spencer King, who had created the Range-Rover in 1970. Here the author tries one in wintry conditions in mid Wales.*

Below: *Part of the 8800 order that will see new Land-Rovers join the British Army until at least 2000. XD 90, 110 and 130 ambulance versions of the Defender are shown.*

section viable the government persuaded British Aerospace to acquire the whole of Rover in 1988. At that time it was estimated that 70 per cent of the 1.6 million Land-Rovers built since 1948 were still in use.

The Discovery, launched in November 1989, had sophisticated Range-Rover type running gear allied to modern styling to bridge the gap between estate cars and Japanese 4 x 4s that spent most of their time on the road. The Discovery halted Land-Rover's slipping sales and output in 1990 was the highest for fifteen years at 66,185. This was helped by Rover's own 2.5 TDi diesel that replaced the VM unit previously imported (and now used by Jeep and others). The new engine gave 25 per cent more speed and 25 per cent more torque, yet used 25 per cent less fuel. In 1994 it developed into the 111 bhp 300 TDi, though

meanwhile some Discovery models had received 2 litre T16 petrol engines as found in the Rover 800.

British Aerospace forged technical and manufacturing links with Honda and late in 1993 the Discovery was launched through the Verno dealership chain in Japan as the Honda Crossroad. From 1989 the 3.5 litre V8 used in all three types of Land-Rover was available in 3.9 litre form. The traditional 'working' models had been renamed Defender for 1991 and forty-eight of the 110 types were soon working alongside Hummers in the US Army as special operations vehicles, where their slimmer girth suited air-portability. This led to the relaunch of the traditional Land-Rover in the United States after an absence of eighteen years.

The Range-Rover was moved increasingly

The first official view of the Freelander released by Land-Rover in March 1997, though the car will not be seen by the public until the Frankfurt Motor Show in September 1997. Petrol and diesel three- and five-door versions are to be produced in 1998.

up-market with a 4.2 litre version in the Vogue LSE of 1992. This developed 200 bhp and had electric air suspension. At the other end of the scale a 200 TDi version was driven from John o'Groats to Land's End at an average speed of 41 mph (66 km/h) with a creditable 53 mpg (18.7 km/litre) fuel consumption.

In 1994 the Discovery was launched in the United States and nine thousand Land-Rover employees were making 1200 Discoveries, 280 Range-Rovers and 470 Defenders per week. Total output was 94,716 in the year, which included part of an order for 640 Range-Rovers for Virgin Atlantic to chauffeur VIP clients.

Early in 1994 BMW acquired the Rover Group from British Aerospace for £800 million and launched a five-year £1.5 billion investment package.

Under development for years with the

codename 'Pegasus', the all-new Range-Rover was launched in September 1994 with increased space, luxury and the option of a 2.5 litre six-cylinder BMW turbo diesel. The petrol V8 engines were revised at the time in 4 and 4.6 litre versions developing up to 225 bhp for a 125 mph (200 km/h) top speed and 0-60 mph (0-96 km/h) in 9.3 seconds. The traditional style of Range-Rover lasted to February 1996, by when employment at Solihull had grown to eleven thousand (all car output having been transferred to Cowley and Longbridge during the 1980s to leave Land-Rover dedicated solely to 4 x 4).

An order for 840 Defenders from the Carabinieri was followed by a massive Italian Army order and then, just as Land-Rover entered the Chinese market, it received its biggest ever single order. This was for 8800 vehicles for the British Army to be supplied up to the year 2000.

The only area of the 4 x 4 on/off-road spectrum currently unrepresented by Land-Rover is the lightweight, compact market dominated by Daihatsu, Suzuki and others, and this is being addressed with a completely new vehicle, codenamed CB40, scheduled for quantity production from 1998. This fashionable and competitively priced range is anticipated to increase Land-rover sales to 200,000 per year at the turn of the century.

The first ever Range-Rover from 1970 in the foreground with a Range-Rover Classic behind and the all-new 1994 model in the background. Like all Land-Rovers, and virtually none of their rivals, bodywork is in corrosion-proof aluminium alloy.

Developed from 1959, and available from 1963, the Volvo Laplander or Valpen (Puppy) used the B18A 68 bhp car engine. Since the mid 1950s Volvo had made some 4 x 4 radio and command cars similar to Humbers for the Swedish Army.

THE POSTWAR JEEP AND ITS RIVALS

It was not just the Rover Company that saw scope for a Jeep-type vehicle after the war. Several other British firms toyed with the idea and the complex Austin Champ reached production for the Army. In Germany the Universal Motor Gerat appeared in 1948 and so impressed Daimler Benz that the design was acquired in 1951 and used to create the multi-purpose Unimog.

In the United States Willys-Overland introduced its peacetime Jeep CJ series; it was taken over by Henry J. Kaiser, becoming Willys Motors Incorporated in 1952. Subsequently the Kaiser Jeep Corporation, it merged with American Motors (AMC) in 1970 and thus joined a group whose predecessors had been responsible for the famous Quad of First World War origin. AMC's Rambler division had previously supplied Jeep with its more powerful engines, though some had also come from Buick

Just as the Land-Rover evolved from a spartan vehicle, so did the Jeep into ever more refined models that were equally at home on the highway. Jeeps have been made under licence in numerous countries, notably by Hotchkiss in France, Beijing in China, Mahindra and Mahindra in India, Viasa in Spain, Mitsubishi in Japan and even Ford of Canada for military purposes.

In 1978 Renault began to build up a stake in AMC and soon gained management control of both the car and Jeep divisions, though in 1987 it was announced that Chrysler would buy AMC.

As well as Mitsubishi and its version of the Jeep, Nissan made a near carbon-copy from the early 1950s, as did Toyota. Both these, and other Japanese motor firms, later developed improved designs and in the early 1970s started to tap a world-wide demand for smaller 4 x 4s, as typified by the Suzuki

LJ10 Jimny. Steyr-Daimler-Puch had been working to the same ends in Austria since 1959 with its Haflinger forward-control miniature 4 x 4, but high prices limited sales volumes.

In the United States Jeep was challenged from 1961 by International Harvester with its Scout, and even Ford returned to the fray with first a Jeep-like MUTT military vehicle in the 1950s and then the civilian Bronco in 1965. General Motors made 4 x 4 pick-ups and estate cars from 1969 and Dodge in the Chrysler Group continued to make Power Wagons reminiscent of its wartime 4 x 4s, before developing its modern Ramcharger in 1974.

Numerous car firms tried their luck in the 4 x 4 field. Alfa Romeo and Fiat made examples from the early 1950s; Austin made the civilian Gipsy from 1957 when its Champ (inherited from Nuffield) had reached the end of the road. From 1955, the Auto-Union Munga gave 4 x 4 experience to Volkswagen when it took over the firm. Four-wheel drive versions of Citroens, Renaults and Peugeots were offered from the early 1950s. Numerous Russian factories built 4 x 4 utilities, military vehicles and even off-road versions of the Pobieda car in the mid 1950s. Volvo made 4 x 4 cars in the same era, followed by a fully off-road forward-control 4 x 4 from 1959. The list of models is long and includes far more names if the efforts of agricultural, military

and other specialist firms like Stonefield are included. Their products range from diminutive all-terrain vehicles powered by air-cooled motorcycle engines up to enormous trucks for hauling oilfield equipment.

At one time the requirements of many 4 x 4 operators could be met by ex-military vehicles but changes in procurement policy and the length of time since a major conflict has meant that demand greatly exceeds supply. Thus sales of new 4 x 4 vehicles are on the increase for commercial purposes at the same time that there has been a vast growth in 4 x 4 leisure and fun motoring.

This started with the beach buggy craze of the 1960s. These 4 x 2 Volkswagen based vehicles, most of American origin, had good off-road ability due, in part, to clever tyre design (that later spread to 4 x 4 vehicles). This fuelled demand for something more robust from hunters, fishermen and lovers of the outdoors who simply wanted to get off the beaten track. 'Fun' versions of the Jeep and other American 4 x 4s met the requirements of some, but the cheaper and more compact Japanese Suzukis and Daihatsus of the 1970s opened up a much greater demand.

The traditionalists were taken by surprise when this same trend spread to Europe, where the typical buyers of 4 x 4s such as the Land-Rover were soon offered a bewildering assortment of rivals, most of which lacked the

The Ford Military Utility Tactical Truck (MUTT) was an updated version of the wartime Jeep that was developed in the 1950s and produced from 1960 by Ford, and later by Kaiser Jeep and AM General. Ford entered the civilian 4 x 4 market in 1965 with the Bronco.

27

Willys quickly converted its production to civilian versions of the wartime Jeep and soon had more 'civilised' and comfortable versions available, including the Utility Wagon and nine-passenger Traveller. This one was used in South Africa.

The Austin Gipsy arrived in 1957 and at first was unusual in having Flexitor rubber independent front suspension. However, in certain conditions independent supension can cause both wheels to retract simultaneously and reduce ground clearance, so when this example was offered in 1962 a conventionally sprung beam front axle was available.

Russia had a particular need for vehicles suitable for primitive provincial roads. With few buyers of 'pleasure' cars, it was able to concentrate on all-wheel driven 'official' and quasi-military vehicles from the Second World War. Of numerous types built, this is a 1964 ZAZ 969 with air-cooled V4 petrol engine. Best known in the West in more recent years are the commercially available Russian Lada Niva and the Romanian Dacia light utility.

The Audi Quattro of 1980 onwards was the first sophisticated 4 x 4 sporting saloon to be generally available at a comparable price to 4 x 2 rivals. It became an unbeatable rally car that led to the widespread use of all-wheel drive in this branch of motor sport. A 1986 coupé rally car is shown here on the sort of loose stage in which it excelled.

Suzuki made its name with motorcycles but began to make cars in 1955 and diminutive 4 x 4s in the early 1970s. Thirty thousand of its SJ range had been sold in Britain by the end of 1986. An SJ 410 VB van is shown here. Suzuki's Spanish-built Vitara range arrived in 1979 and by 1995 some 2.5 million Suzuki 4 x 4s had been built overall, including a new Mazda 2 litre diesel-engined model.

29

Above left: *Originally known by the unkind name of Brat in 1978, the 4 x 4 Subaru pick-up had become the 1800 MV when this photograph was taken in 1981. An unusual feature was a horizontally opposed four-cylinder engine.*

Above right: *Having made Jeep-type FJ and BJ utility vehicles in the 1950s, Toyota developed more general-purpose Land-Cruisers in the 1970s, like this station wagon with a 3.9 litre six-cylinder truck engine. 120,000 Land-Cruisers were built per year at the time, with 95 per cent for export.*

lasting qualities of aluminium alloy but were cheaper and more freely available.

The days of the disposable 4 x 4 had arrived and Rover saw sales of its Land-Rover decline whilst its Range-Rover sales grew dramatically to approximately a half of output. To some buyers the superiority of the Range-Rover was not as important as its image, and these same clients for glamorous on- and off-road vehicles soon found alternatives in the Mitsubishi Shogun, Isuzu Trooper and Mercedes-Benz G Wagen of the 1980s. The G Wagen was built by Steyr-Daimler-Puch, which had earlier made the Haflinger, the Pinzgauer and other in-genious vehicles and had become a 4 x 4 technical centre providing designs for Fiat and Volkswagen.

Though Jeep, Land-Rover, Dodge Power Wagon and Toyota Land-Cruiser opened up the light 4 x 4 market there are numerous other contenders in the 1990s, including Korea's Ssang Yong Musso and Asia Rocsta. Vauxhall adopted its GM colleague Isuzu's Monterey and also developed the Frontera, whilst Ford's Maverick and Nissan's Terrano are virtually identical products from Spain. Most of the others are Japanese apart from the Jeep, now produced for Europe in the United States and in an Austrian factory.

As part of its avowed intent to offer all its vehicles with four-wheel drive in 1985 Volkswagen Audi launched a Syncro version of the rear-engined Transporter. This has an FFD coupling (called Visco by Volkswagen) to bring in front-wheel drive automatically when required. Volkswagen and Steyr-Daimler-Puch collaborated in the vehicle's manufacture.

Above: *Vauxhall's petrol or diesel Frontera arrived in 1991 in a joint venture between General Motors and Isuzu, and here one is assembled at the IBC factory in Luton. Vauxhall subsequently also sold the larger Japanese Isuzu Trooper 4 x 4, calling it the Monterey. The Trooper itself is also available from the importers of the Korean Ssang Yong 4 x 4.*

Top right: *Mitsubushi's well-known Shogun was available in Britain from mid 1983 under the brand name Colt. This is one of the first, since when sophistication and price have increased. Top of the range 3.5 litre 24 valve 205 bhp in 1995 cost £35,000.*

Bottom right: *Ford's Maverick, available from the summer of 1993, was built in Nissan's Barcelona factory. This had once been home to Ebro, which had made Jeeps under licence. Shown is a short-wheelbase Maverick with choice of 2.4 litre petrol or 2.7 litre diesel engine. For 1997 the American-built 4 litre V6 Explorer was added to Ford's UK line-up. Since its introduction in 1990 two million had been sold, making it 'the most popular sports-utility model in the world' according to Ford.*

MAGAZINES AND CLUBS

There is a range of magazines covering 4 x 4 vehicles. These include: *Land-Rover International, Land-Rover World, International Off-Roader, Off-Road and 4 Wheel Drive, Diesel Car and 4 x 4,* plus various club publications. There are numerous books past and present on 4 x 4 vehicles available from bookshops and auto-jumbles.

Clubs include:
Quattro Owners Club: c/o AM Cars, 11/12 Willoughby Place, Chard, Somerset TA2 2CC.
All Wheel Drive Club: Public Relations Officer, Dave Hill, Peartree House, Hatton Lane, Warrington, Cheshire WA4 4BY.
Austin Gipsy Register: Mike Gilbert, 24 Green Close, Sturminster Newton, Dorset DT10 1BJ.
Land-Rover Series 2 Club: PO Box 1750, Bridport, Dorset.
Land-Rover Series One Club: David Bowyer, East Foldhay, Zeal Monachorum, Crediton, Devon EX17 6DH.
Range-Rover Register: Secretary, Les Booth, 94 Rainham Road, Rainham, Kent ME8 7UD.
Association of Rover Clubs: A. J. Stavordale, 65 Longmead Avenue, Hazel Grove, Stockport, Cheshire SK7 5PJ.

PLACES TO VISIT

As well as numerous off-road trials and events organised by clubs during most weekends of the year there are the following permanent displays. These museums are believed to have 4 x 4 and related vehicles on exhibition. Intending visitors are advised to find out times of opening before making a special journey.

Airborne Forces Museum, Browning Barracks, Queens Avenue, Aldershot, Hampshire GU11 2BU. Telephone: 01252 346919.

British Commercial Vehicle Museum, King Street, Leyland, Preston, Lancashire PR5 1LE. Telephone: 01772 451011.

Glasgow Museum of Transport, Kelvin Hall, Bunhouse Road, Glasgow G3 8DP. Telephone: 0141-221 9600.

Haynes Motor Museum, Sparkford, near Yeovil, Somerset BA22 7LH. Telephone: 01963 440804.

Heritage Motor Centre, Banbury Road, Gaydon, Warwickshire CV35 0BJ. Telephone: 01926 641188.

Museum of British Road Transport, St Agnes Lane, Hales Street, Coventry, West Midlands CV1 1PN. Telephone: 01203 832425.

National Motor Museum, John Montagu Building, Beaulieu, Brockenhurst, Hampshire SO42 7ZN. Telephone: 01590 612345.

Science Museum, Exhibition Road, South Kensington, London SW7 2DD. Telephone: 0171-938 8000. Also at Wroughton Airfield, near Swindon, Wiltshire SN4 9NS. Telephone: 01793 814446.

Tank Museum, Bovington Camp, near Wareham, Dorset BH20 6JG. Telephone: 01929 405096.

Ulster Folk and Transport Museum, Cultra Manor, Holywood, County Down BT18 0EU. Telephone: 01232 428428.

In May 1996 Essex Constabulary acquired six Jeep Cherokee 4.0 Limited vehicles capable of 112 mph (180 km/h). By that date 18,000 new Jeeps had been sold in Britain since their relaunch in the early 1970s. Five British police forces use Jeeps but the number of these vehicles falls far short of the one thousand plus police Land-Rovers, which cover 10 million miles (16 million km) annually.